Electricity and Magnetism Experiments

Using Batteries, Bulbs, Wires, and More

One Hour or Less Science Experiments

LAST MINUTE Science Projects

ROBERT GARDNER

Enslow Publishers, Inc.
40 Industrial Road
Box 398
Berkeley Heights, NJ 07922
USA

http://www.enslow.com

Library of Congress Cataloging-in-Publication Data

Gardner, Robert, 1929–
    Electricity and magnetism experiments using batteries, bulbs, wires, and more : one hour or less sci-
ence experiments / Robert Gardner.
        p. cm. — (Last-minute science projects)
    Includes index.
    Summary: "Find out how to make a compass, an electromagnet, a parallel circuit, and many other
quick science projects using electricity and magnetism"—Provided by publisher.
    ISBN 978-0-7660-3960-5
    1. Electricity—Experiments—Juvenile literature. I. Title.
    QC527.2.G3824 2012
    537.078—dc22
                                            2011007628

Future editions
Paperback ISBN 978-1-4644-0145-9
EPUB ISBN 978-1-4645-1052-6
PDF ISBN 978-1-4646-1052-3

Printed in the United States of America04

042012 Lake Book Manufacturing, Inc., Melrose Park, IL

10 9 8 7 6 5 4 3 2 1

To Our Readers: We have done our best to make sure all Internet Addresses in this book were active and
appropriate when we went to press. However, the author and the publisher have no control over and assume no
liability for the material available on those Internet sites or on other Web sites they may link to. Any comments
or suggestions can be sent by e-mail to comments@enslow.com or to the address on the back cover.

Illustration Credits: © 2011 by Stephen Rountree (www.rountreegraphics.com), pp. 13 (b), 17,
21, 25, 31, 33, 35, 37 (a), 38, 41, 43; Shutterstock.com, pp. 1, 3, 4; Tom LaBaff, pp. 9, 11, 37
(b, c); Tom LaBaff and Stephanie LaBaff, pp. 13 (a), 15, 19, 23, 27, 29.

Cover Photos: Shutterstock.com

Contents

LAST MINUTE Science Projects

SEP 2012

🎗 Contains ideas for more science fair projects.

Are You Running Late?

Maybe you have a science project due tomorrow and you've put it off until now. What can you do? This book provides a solution! Here you will find electrical and magnetic experiments that you can do in one hour or less. In fact, some of them can be done in 30 minutes, others in 15 minutes, and some in as little as 5 minutes. Even if you have plenty of time to prepare for your next science project or science fair, or are just looking for some fun science experiments, you can enjoy this book, too.

Each experiment is followed by a "Keep Exploring" section. There you will find ideas for projects or experiments in which the details are left to you. You can design and carry out your own experiments, **under adult supervision**, when you have more time.

Sometimes you may need a partner to help you. Work with someone who likes to do experiments as much as you do. Then you will both enjoy what you are doing. **If any safety issues are involved in doing an experiment, you will be warned or asked to work with an adult.** Don't take any chances that could lead to an injury.

Like any good scientist, you will find it useful to record your ideas, notes, data, and conclusions in a notebook. You will be able to refer to things you have done, which will help you with future experiments.

The Scientific Method

Different sciences use different ways of experimenting. Depending on the problem, one method is likely to be better than another. Designing a new medicine for heart disease and finding evidence of water on Mars require different experiments.

Even with these differences, most scientists use the scientific method. This includes: making an observation, coming up with a question, making a hypothesis (a possible answer to the question) and a prediction (an if-then statement), designing and conducting an experiment, analyzing results, drawing conclusions, and deciding if the hypothesis is true or false. Scientists share their results. They publish articles in science journals.

Once you have a question, you can make a hypothesis. Your hypothesis is a possible answer to the question (what you think will happen). For example, you might hypothesize that for an electric circuit to work, one end of the circuit must be connected to the positive pole of a battery while the other end is connected to the negative pole. Then you test your hypothesis.

In most cases you should do a controlled experiment. This means having two groups that are treated the same except for the thing being tested. That thing is called a variable. To test the hypothesis above, you might have two circuits with a light bulb, wires, and a battery. You would connect the bulb in one circuit to opposite poles of a battery. In the other circuit you might connect both sides of the bulb to the same pole. If the bulb lights when connected to opposite poles, you would say that your hypothesis is true.

The results of one experiment often lead to another question. Or they may send you off in another direction. Whatever the results, something can be learned from every experiment!

Science Fairs

All of the investigations in this book contain ideas that might lead you to a science fair project. However, judges at science fairs do not reward projects or experiments that are simply copied from a book. For example, a diagram of a battery would not impress most judges; however, a unique method of using electricity to determine the charge on metal ions would be likely to gain their attention.

Science fair judges tend to reward creative thought and imagination. It is difficult to be creative or imaginative unless you are really interested in your project. Therefore, try to choose an investigation that excites you. And before you jump into a project, consider, too, your own talents and the cost of the materials you will need.

If you decide to use an experiment or idea found in this book for a science fair, find ways to modify or extend it. This should not be difficult. As you do investigations, you will get new ideas. You will think of questions that experiments can answer. The experiments will make great science fair projects because the ideas are your own and are interesting to you.

Your Notebook

Your notebook, as any scientist will tell you, is a valuable possession. It should contain ideas you may have as you experiment, sketches you may draw, calculations you may make, and hypotheses you may suggest. It should include a description of every experiment you do, the data you record, such as voltages, currents, resistors, weights, and so on. It should also contain the results of your experiments, graphs you draw, and any conclusions you may be able to reach based on your results.

Safety First

1. Do any experiments or projects, whether from this book or of your own design, **under the adult supervision** of a science teacher or other knowledgeable adult.

2. Read all instructions carefully before proceeding with a project. If you have questions, check with your supervisor before going any further.

3. **Always wear safety goggles** when doing experiments that could cause particles to enter your eyes. Tie back long hair and wear shoes that cover your feet completely.

4. Do not eat or drink while experimenting. Never taste substances being used (unless instructed to do so).

5. Never let water droplets come in contact with a hot light bulb.

6. Never experiment with household electricity. Instead, use batteries.

7. Use only alcohol-based thermometers. Older thermometers may contain mercury, which is a dangerous substance. It is dangerous to touch mercury or breathe mercury vapor, and such thermometers have been banned in many states. If you have a mercury thermometer in the house, **ask an adult** if it can be taken to a local thermometer exchange location.

8. Maintain a serious attitude while conducting experiments. Never engage in horseplay or play practical jokes.

9. At the end of every activity, clean all materials used and put them away. Then wash your hands thoroughly with soap and water.

60 min

Here are experiments with electricity and magnets that you can do in one hour or less. You don't have any time to lose, so let's get started!

1 Finding the North and South Poles of Magnets

WHAT YOU NEED:
- thread
- tape
- 2 bar magnets or 2 square or circular ceramic magnets
- masking tape
- pen
- magnetic compass

What's the Plan?

Let's find the north and south poles of two magnets.

What You Do

1. Using thread and tape, hang two bar or flat magnets far from one another and far from any metallic objects (Figure 1).

2. Wait until the magnets stop turning. One end or side (the north pole) will be northernmost. The south pole will be on the south end or side.

3. Using masking tape and a pen, mark an "N" on the magnet's north end or side. Mark an "S" on the other end or side.

4. Repeat the marking process on the second magnet.

5. Bring the north poles of the two magnets near one another. Watch them repel each other.

6. Bring the north pole of one magnet near the south pole of the second magnet. Watch them attract.

7. Bring the south poles of the magnets close together. Watch them repel.

8. A magnetic compass is a small magnet that is free to turn. Slowly bring the north pole of one magnet near the north pole of a compass. Watch the compass needle be repelled.

9. Slowly bring the south pole of one magnet near the north pole of a compass needle. Watch the attraction.

What's Going On?

A magnet free to turn will soon come to rest. One end (or side, if flat) will "point" north. That end or side is the magnet's north pole. Its south pole will be on the other end or side. As you have seen, like magnetic poles repel. Opposite (N and S) poles attract.

Keep Exploring—If You Have More Time!

Obtain several square or circular ceramic magnets with holes in their centers. Can you make these magnets "float" above one another on a stick or a soda straw?

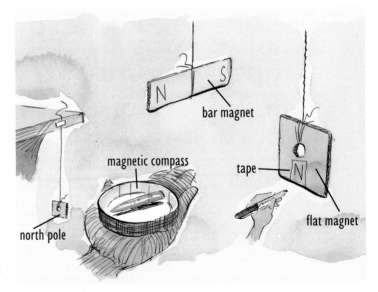

Figure 1. Finding the north and south poles of bar or flat magnets.

9

2 Is It Magnetic?

What's the Plan?

Let's see which objects in your home are magnets, magnetic matter, or nonmagnetic matter.

What You Do

1. Obtain a magnet. Then gather a variety of objects. Include another magnet as well as items such as coins, paper, nails, copper wire, iron wire, aluminum foil, plastic and glass objects, chalk, brass, rubber bands or erasers, wooden pencils, paper clips, and other common objects.

2. Bring the magnet near each of the various objects you collected (Figure 2). Divide them into three groups: (A) Magnets: Magnets will be attracted by one pole of the magnet and repelled by the other. (B) Magnetic matter: Things attracted to both poles of the magnet. (C) Nonmagnetic matter: Things not affected by either pole of the magnet.

WHAT YOU NEED:

- 2 magnets
- coins
- paper
- pen or pencil
- nails
- copper wire
- iron wire
- aluminum foil
- plastic and glass objects
- chalk
- brass object
- rubber bands
- erasers
- wooden pencil
- paper clips
- other common objects

What's Going On?

Magnets attract and repel other magnets. Unlike a true magnet, magnetic matter is attracted to either pole of a magnet. Once the attracting magnet is removed, the matter will not act like a magnet. Nonmagnetic matter is not affected by a magnet.

Keep Exploring—If You Have More Time!

Will a magnet attract magnetic matter or another magnet if other matter is between them? You might try putting paper, glass, plastic, wood, water, and aluminum foil between them. How about a tin can lid?

Figure 2. Which things are magnets? Nonmagnets? Magnetic matter?

3 Does It Conduct Electricity?

What's the Plan?

Let's find out which things conduct electricity (conductors) and which don't (nonconductors).

What You Do

1. Collect items such as those listed in the "What You Need" section.

2. Set up the electrical circuit shown in Figure 3a. Figure 3b uses simple lines and symbols to represent the circuit items seen in Figure 3a. A strong, wide rubber band can be used to hold the ends of the wires against opposite poles of a D-cell.

3. Test one object at a time by touching the wires labeled 1 and 2 to opposite sides of the object. If the bulb lights, the object is a conductor. If it doesn't glow, you have a nonconductor or a poor conductor.

4. Make a list of conductors and nonconductors. Can you make any conclusions?

WHAT YOU NEED:

- solid objects such as coins, nails, paper clips, plastic, glass, wood, paper, wax, chalk, etc.
- battery holder
- flashlight bulb
- D-cell
- 3 insulated wires with clips
- bulb holder

What's Going On?

Electricity is made up of positive and negative charges. In some ways, electric charges are similar to magnetic poles. Positive charges attract negative charges and repel positive charges; negative charges attract positive charges and repel negative charges.

Negative charges (electrons) moving along a wire is called an *electric current*. An electric current makes a light bulb glow. *Conductors* allow an electric current to flow (move) through them. *Nonconductors* do not.

Keep Exploring—If You Have More Time!

Liquids, such as water, salt water, alcohol, household ammonia, vinegar, carbonated sodas, and cooking oil, might also be tested for conductivity. Design an experiment to test liquids. (A 6-volt lantern battery is best for testing liquids.)

a)

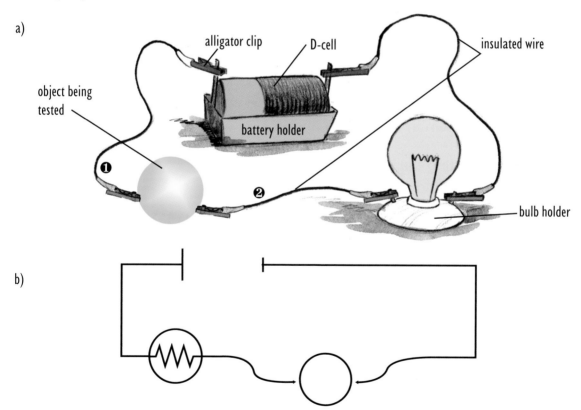

b)

Figure 3. a) Arrangement used to test objects for electrical conductivity. b) Symbols can show this circuit.

4 Make a Simple Series Circuit

What's the Plan?
Let's build a series circuit.

What You Do

1. Build the series circuit shown in Figure 4a. A series circuit is one in which two or more circuit elements, such as light bulbs, are arranged one after the other as shown in Figure 4a. To build a series circuit, it is convenient to have holders for the bulbs and battery. If you have bulb and battery holders, you can use them. If not, you can make ones like those shown in Figures 4b and 4c.

2. After connecting the wires shown to a D-cell, both bulbs should glow.

3. Remove one of the bulbs. What happens?

4. Replace the bulb. Both bulbs will glow again.

5. Remove the other bulb. What happens?

What's Going On?
Removing either bulb opens the circuit. It prevents electric current from being conducted through the bulb to the rest of the circuit.

WHAT YOU NEED:

- 2 bulb holders, perhaps made by you
- 2 battery holders, perhaps made by you
- 2 flashlight bulbs
- 1 D-cell
- 2 soft wood blocks
- 2 thumb tacks
- 2 paper clips
- strong wide rubber band
- masking tape
- 2 or 3 insulated wires with alligator clips (2 if you make your own holders)
- 3 short lengths of bare copper wire to connect bulbs together and to connect to wires from the D-cell

Keep Exploring—If You Have More Time!

- Build a circuit with three bulbs in series. How does the brightness of the bulbs change when more bulbs are put in series?

- How many bulbs in series are needed for the bulbs to emit no light? Does that mean there is no electric current? How can you find out?

- Invent and build some bulb and battery holders of your own design.

- Many household circuits have two switches, one at each end of a hall for example. Use wires, a flashlight bulb, and a D-cell to make a model of a circuit that can be turned on or off at either of two switches.

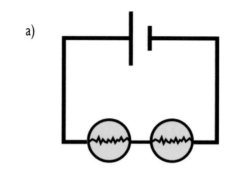

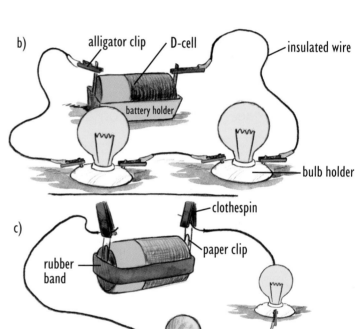

Figure 4 a) A way to represent two lightbulbs in series connected to a D-cell (1.5 volts). b) Circuit with a homemade battery holder. c) Circuit with a homemade bulb holder.

30 Minutes or Less

Really pressed for time? Here are some experiments you can do in 30 minutes or less.

5 Seeing a Magnetic Field

What's the Plan?

Map the magnetic field around a bar magnet.

What You Do

1. Place a bar magnet on a wooden surface. Put a sheet of white cardboard on the magnet.

2. Sprinkle iron filings on the cardboard. Tap the cardboard gently with your finger. You will see the magnetic field's pattern emerge.

3. You can also map the field with a compass or compasses. Place the magnet on a sheet of paper. Put the compass or compasses at various places around the magnet. Draw an arrowhead just in front of the north-seeking pole of the compass needle. This is the direction of the field. Draw a dash just behind the arrow. After you do this a number of times, the magnetic field pattern can be seen.

WHAT YOU NEED:

- bar magnet

- wooden surface

- sheet of white cardboard about 30 cm (12 in) square or a sheet of white paper taped to cardboard

- iron filings (borrow from your school or make them by filing steel nails or by cutting steel wool into very short lengths)

- one or more magnetic compasses

- paper and pencil

What's Going On?

The magnetic field around one magnet exerts forces on other magnets. Iron filings "feel" these forces. They line up in the direction of the field. Even though magnetic fields are invisible, you can map them. In Figure 5, the magnetic field around a bar magnet is revealed by many small compasses. It should be similar to the field you drew. Each compass shows the direction of the magnetic field. The direction of the field at any point is the direction given by the north pole of a compass needle.

The idea of magnetic fields and their mapping was introduced by Michael Faraday (1791–1867), a great English scientist.

Keep Exploring—If You Have More Time!

- Figure out a way to map the magnetic field around a bar magnet in three-dimensions.

- Which part of a bar magnet is stronger, the poles or the middle? Do an experiment to find out.

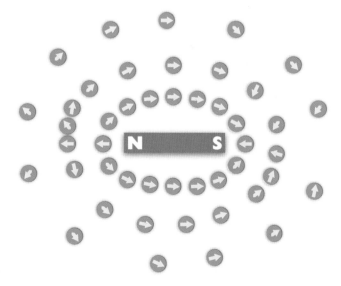

Figure 5. The magnetic field around a bar magnet. The field is revealed by a number of magnetic compasses. Tiny compasses (iron filings) provide even better detail.

6 Make a Parallel Circuit

WHAT YOU NEED:

- D-cell

- 4 wires, preferably with alligator clips

- 2 identical flashlight bulbs

- 2 bulb holders (homemade or bought)

- 1 battery holder (homemade or bought)

What's the Plan?

Let's make a parallel circuit. Bulbs connected one after the other, as shown in Figure 6a, are in a series circuit. But bulbs can also be connected in a parallel (side-by-side) circuit as shown in Figure 6b.

What You Do

1. Gather a D-cell, wires, two bulbs, and bulb and battery holders. (To build your own bulb and battery holders, see Figure 4.)

2. Build the parallel circuit shown in Figure 6b. As you can see, the brightness of the two bulbs is very nearly the same.

3. Remove one of the bulbs. The other bulb will continue to glow.

What's Going On?

In the parallel circuit with two bulbs, one bulb will continue to light when the second is removed. The glowing bulb is still connected to both poles of the D-cell. When you remove one bulb in a series circuit (as you did in Experiment 4), the circuit is opened. No current can flow.

Keep Exploring—If You Have More Time!

- Are the circuits in your home wired in series or in parallel? What makes you think so?

- How does the brightness of two bulbs in series compare with the brightness of two bulbs in parallel if both circuits are connected to one D-cell? Can you explain why?

- Build a parallel circuit with two bulbs. Add switches so that either or both bulbs can be turned off. How is this like the circuits in your home?

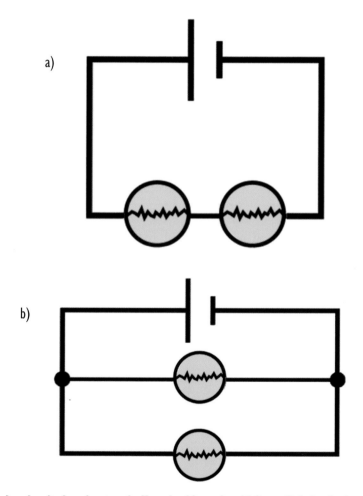

a)

b)

Figure 6. a) A series circuit showing two bulbs wired in series. b) A parallel circuit showing two bulbs wired in parallel.

7 Build an Electric Current Meter

What's the Plan?
Let's use a compass to build a meter that can detect electric currents.

What You Do

1. To make the meter, wind about 4 m (13 ft) of 24-gauge insulated (enameled) wire around a compass, making a coil as shown in Figure 7.

2. Use tape to keep the wire coils together. Leave about 15 cm (6 in) of wire at each end of the coil.

3. Using sandpaper, remove about 3 cm (1 in) of insulation from the ends of the coil.

4. Use clay to hold the coil and compass in place.

5. Arrange the coil so the wires are parallel to the compass needle as shown.

6. Briefly connect the two ends of the wire coil to opposite poles of a D-cell. The compass needle will turn. As you can see, the meter can detect an electric current.

WHAT YOU NEED:
- 4 m (13 ft) of 24-gauge insulated (enameled) wire
- magnetic compass
- tape
- ruler
- sandpaper
- clay
- D-cell

What's Going On?
An electric current moving through a wire creates a magnetic field that encircles the wire. The magnetic field will make a compass needle turn.

Keep Exploring—If You Have More Time!

- Turn the D-cell around so that current flows in the opposite direction. Predict the direction the compass needle will turn after making this change. Were you right?

- Does the needle deflect as much if you connect it to a circuit that has a flashlight bulb in it? How much does it deflect if there are two flashlight bulbs in series? Three? Four? Suppose you place enough bulbs in series so that the bulbs do not glow. Will the meter still detect a current?

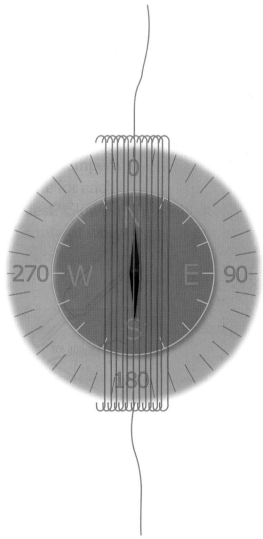

Figure 7. You can build an electric current meter.

8 Making Magnetic Coils

What's the Plan?

Magnets form when electric currents move through coils of wire. Let's make this type of magnet.

WHAT YOU NEED:

- ruler and scissors
- 10 m (33 ft) of #24 enamel-coated copper wire
- 2 D-cells
- tape
- sandpaper
- magnetic compass

What You Do

1. Cut two 5-m (16-ft) lengths from a coil of #24 enamel-coated copper wire.

2. Wind each length of wire into a coil by wrapping it around a D-cell (Figure 8a).

3. Slide each coil of wire off the D-cell. Wrap small pieces of tape around the coils to hold the wires in place. Leave about 30 cm (1 ft) of wire uncoiled at each end. These uncoiled end wires will be used to connect the coils to D-cells.

4. Using sandpaper, remove about 3 cm (1 in) of enamel insulation from each end of the uncoiled wires.

5. Attach one coil to a D-cell (Figure 8b). A current will flow through the coil. Don't leave the coil connected very long or you will wear out the D-cell!

6. With the coil hanging from a D-cell, bring a magnetic compass close to each side of the coil. The compass needle's north pole will point away from the coil's north pole. It will be attracted by the coil's south pole.

7. Attach the second coil to another D-cell. Hold the faces of these two coils close together as shown in Figure 8c. The coils will either attract or repel one another. Turn one around and they will do the opposite.

What's Going On?

Because there is a magnetic field around an electric current, a coil of wire carrying a current will behave like a magnet, as shown in Figure 8d.

Keep Exploring—If You Have More Time!

Figure out a way to use a ceramic magnet, a D-cell, and a small wire coil to make a tiny electric motor.

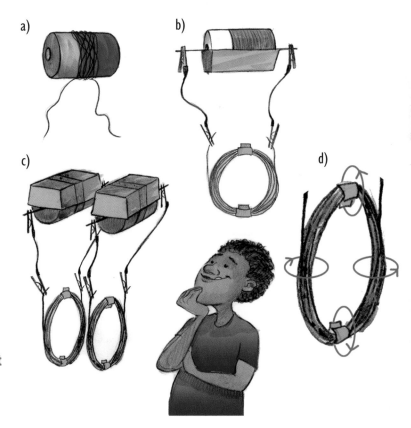

a)

b)

c)

d)

Figure 8. a) Make wire coils by wrapping wire around a D-cell.
b) Connect the ends of a coil to a D-cell.
c) What happens if two coils carrying electric currents are brought near one another?
d) The magnetic field goes around a coil carrying an electric current.

9 Generate Electricity with a Magnet

What's the Plan?

Michael Faraday generated electricity by changing the magnetic field inside a wire coil. So can you.

What You Do

1. Wind 10 meters (33 ft) of 24-gauge insulated (enameled) copper wire around a roll of tape (Figure 9a). Leave about 15 cm (6 in) of wire unwound at each end of the coil.

2. Using sandpaper, remove about 3 cm (1 in) of insulation from the wires at each end of the coil.

3. Using long insulated wires, connect each end of the coil to the poles of a microammeter, a milliammeter, or the electric meter built in Experiment 7.

4. Change the magnetic field in the coil. Move a strong magnet in and out of the coil (Figure 9b). Use either a strong bar magnet or several ceramic magnets joined together. The meter will indicate a current as you move the magnet in and out of the coil.

WHAT YOU NEED:

- 10 meters (33 ft) of #24 enamel-coated copper wire
- roll of duct or masking tape
- sandpaper
- 2 insulated wires
- ruler
- microammeter, milliammeter, or the electric meter built in Experiment 7
- magnet (strong bar magnet or 6 or more ceramic magnets joined together)

5. Push the south pole of the magnet into the coil. The meter's needle moves one way. Pull the magnet out of the coil. The needle moves the opposite way.

6. Push the north pole into the coil. The compass needle turns opposite the direction it turned when the south pole was used.

7. Change the rate at which the magnetic field changes by moving the magnet at different speeds. The faster the magnetic field changes, the larger the current. If you don't move the magnet, there is no current.

What's Going On?

When the magnetic field inside a coil of wire is changing, electric charges (electrons) in the wire are pushed along the wire, creating an electric current.

a) wire — roll of duct or masking tape

Keep Exploring—If You Have More Time!

Can you generate a current by moving the coil while someone holds the magnet still? What does this tell you?

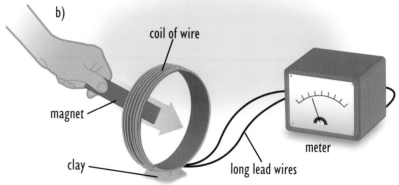

b) coil of wire

magnet

clay

long lead wires

meter

Figure 9. You can generate electricity by changing the magnetic field inside a coil of wire.

25

15 Minutes or Less

Time is really in short supply if you need an experiment you can do in 15 minutes! Here to rescue you are four more experiments you can do quickly.

10 Electricity and Magnetism

What's the Plan?

For years, scientists wondered: Was there a connection between electricity and magnetism? The forces were similar. Like poles repel and unlike poles (N and S) attract; like charges repel and unlike charges (+ and −) attract. In 1819, Hans Christian Øersted, a Danish scientist, discovered the connection. So can you.

WHAT YOU NEED:
- sandpaper
- D-cell
- long enameled copper wire
- magnetic compass

What You Do

1. Use sandpaper to remove 3 cm (1 in) of insulation from each end of a long enameled copper wire.

2. Hold one end of the wire firmly against the negative (−) pole of a D-cell (Figure 10). Place a magnetic compass under the wire. The wire should be parallel to the compass needle as shown.

3. Touch the other end of the wire to the positive end of the D-cell. A current will flow in the wire. The compass needle will turn.

4. Turn the D-cell around so that current flows in the opposite direction. The compass needle will turn in a direction opposite to the direction it turned before.

5. Repeat the experiment with the wire under the compass. The needle will turn opposite the direction it turned before.

What's Going On?

Moving electric charges, such as a current in a wire, create a magnetic field. The field encircles the moving charges in the wire.

Keep Exploring—If You Have More Time!

- Devise a rule that will allow you to predict the direction that a compass needle will turn when above or below a wire carrying a current.

- Find a way to map the magnetic field around a wire that carries an electric current.

Figure 10. Øersted's experiment led to the discovery of a connection between magnetism and electricity.

11 Make an Electromagnet

What's the Plan?

Giant commercial electromagnets are used to lift and move huge piles of scrap metal. You can make a much smaller electromagnet.

What You Do

1. Wrap 100 turns of insulated copper wire around an iron nail. As you start, leave about 10 cm (4 in) of the copper wire unwrapped. Always wrap the wire in the same direction.

2. Leave another 10 cm of the wire unwrapped before cutting any extra wire.

3. Sandpaper away about 3 cm (1 in) of the enamel insulation from the ends of the two 10-cm lengths of wire. Connect the ends of the coil to a D-cell using wires with alligator clips as shown in Figure 11. Use a strong, wide rubber band to hold the clips against the poles of the D-cell. Alterntely, you may use a battery holder like the one in Figure 11.

4. How many steel paper clips can your electromagnet lift? (Don't connect the electromagnet to the battery for very long. The battery will wear out quickly under such conditions.)

WHAT YOU NEED:

- ruler
- about 1 meter (3.3 ft) of #24 enamel-coated copper wire
- iron nail
- sandpaper
- D-cell
- 2 wires with alligator clips
- strong, wide rubber band or battery holder
- steel paper clips

What's Going On?

A wire coil carrying an electric current creates a magnetic field. Placing an iron core (nail) inside the coil makes the magnetic field much stronger.

Keep Exploring—If You Have More Time!

- Rebuild the electromagnet. This time wind half the turns in one direction and the other half in the opposite direction. Predict the number of paper clips your electromagnet will lift now. Were you right? Can you explain what you saw?

- Do an experiment to find out how the number of turns in the coil affects the strength of the electromagnet.

- Can metals other than iron or steel be used as the cores for an electromagnet? Do some experiments to find out. What about nonmetals such as wood or plastic?

Figure 11. You can make an electromagnet.

29

12 Make a Simple Electric Motor

What's the Plan?

Let's use a compass and an electromagnet to make a simple electric motor.

What You Do

1. Connect an electromagnet (see Experiment 11) to a D-cell using a wide rubber band and wires with alligator clips (Figure 12). Don't leave the electromagnet connected for very long. (The D-cell will discharge quickly under these conditions.)

2. Slowly bring the end of the electromagnet near the north pole of the compass as shown in Figure 12. If it repels the compass's north pole, go on to step 3. If it attracts the compass's north pole, move it toward the compass's south pole.

3. Now move the electromagnet toward and away from the pole of the compass so that the compass needle spins like an electric motor.

What's Going On?

The pole of the electromagnet repels the like pole of the compass needle and makes it start to spin. By properly timing your movement of the electromagnet toward the like pole of the compass needle, you can keep the needle spinning like a motor.

In a real electric motor, a device called a commutator automatically causes the coil's current to reverse every half turn. In that way, the motor is kept turning by the repulsion of the poles of the coil and the magnet inside the motor.

Keep Exploring—If You Have More Time!

- Design and build your own electric motor that will turn when connected to a battery.

- Does distance affect the force between the poles of two magnets? Does it affect the force between a magnet and magnetic matter such as paper clips?

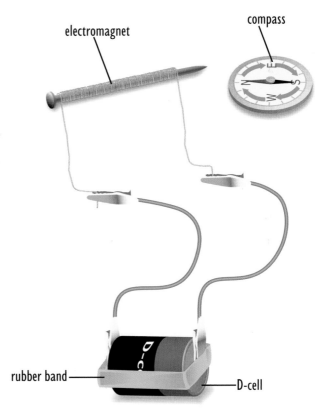

Figure 12. Use an electromagnet and a compass to make a simple electric motor.

13 Make a Fruit and Nails Battery

What's the Plan?

Let's make a simple battery from two nails and a piece of fruit.

What You Do

1. Squeeze a whole lemon to free the liquid inside its skin.

2. Push a copper nail into the lemon. Then push an aluminum or an iron nail into the lemon. The two nails should be an inch or two apart.

3. Use wires with alligator clips to connect the nails to the poles of a microammeter (Figure 13). A microammeter can read very small electric currents (millionths of an ampere). If a microammeter is not available, you can use a galvanometer or the electric meter from Experiment 7. You will see the meter needle move, showing that the battery has produced an electric current.

WHAT YOU NEED:

- lemon
- copper nail
- aluminum or iron nail
- wires with alligator clips
- microammeter or a galvanometer or the electric meter from Experiment 7

What's Going On?

A battery can be made from two different metals and an electrolyte. Charges move from one metal (negative electrode) to the other (positive electrode) and through the electrolyte. An electrolyte is a liquid or pasty substance

through which electric charges can move. This battery used copper and aluminum (or iron) as the two metals. The lemon served as the electrolyte.

Keep Exploring—If You Have More Time!

- Try making a battery from other fruits. You might try an orange, apple, pear, pickle, and olive. Which fruit battery produces the largest electric current?

- Can you make batteries from vegetables such as potatoes, carrots, turnips, and asparagus?

- Design and build an electric generator strong enough to light a flashlight bulb.

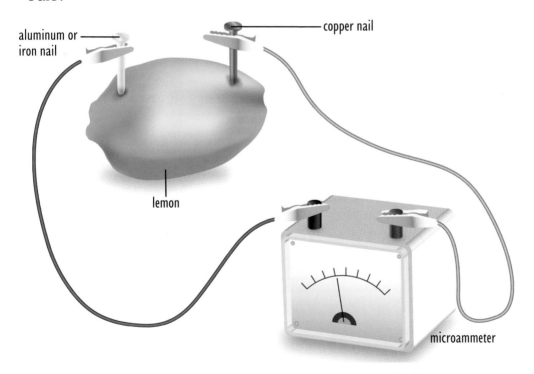

Figure 13. You can make a battery from a piece of fruit.

5 Minutes or Less

Are you desperate? Do you have very little time to prepare a project? If so, you have come to the right place. Here are experiments you can do in five minutes or less.

14 Can You Feel Magnetism?

What's the Plan?

Can you feel magnetism? Let's find out.

WHAT YOU NEED:

- a magnet
- pliers
- steel nail

What You Do

1. Hold a magnet in your hand. Move it over and near sensitive parts of your body—your fingers, cheeks, lips, hands, forearms, ears, etc. (Figure 14a). You will not feel anything.

2. Use pliers to hold a steel nail near the magnet (Figure 14b). You will see that a magnetic force is pulling the nail.

What's Going On?

Have you ever received an electric shock by touching a metal door knob after walking across a rug? If you have, you know electricity can be felt. From your experiment, you know that you don't feel magnetism. However, a nail or any iron-containing object will be attracted to a magnet.

Keep Exploring—If You Have More Time!

- Do some research. Find out how some animals use Earth's magnetic field to navigate. Do you think they feel Earth's magnetic force?

- Where is Earth's north magnetic pole? Where is its south magnetic pole?

- Suppose you held a magnetic compass above Earth's magnetic pole that is in northern Canada. In what direction would the compass needle point? In what direction would it point if held over Earth's magnetic pole in the southern hemisphere? Can you make a model to answer these questions?

- Will the tiny particles in an iron-enriched cereal respond to a magnet?

a)

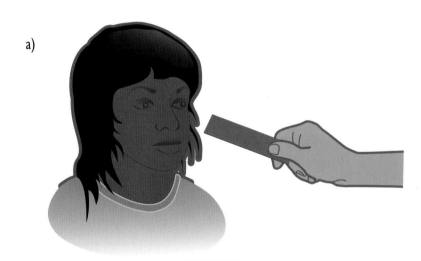

b)

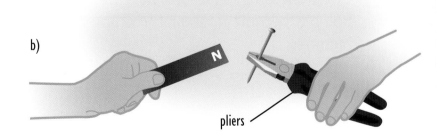

pliers

Figure 14. a) Can you feel magnetism?
b) Can you feel a magnetic force?

15 Make a Magnet from a Nonmagnet

What's the Plan?

Let's see if we can change a nonmagnet (an iron bolt) into a magnet.

What You Do

WHAT YOU NEED:

- iron bolt
- magnetic compass
- hammer

1. First, be sure an iron bolt is not a magnet. Bring it near a compass. It should have little or no effect on the compass needle.

2. Hold the bolt so that it is aligned with Earth's magnetic field. A magnetic compass will show you the direction of Earth's magnetic field. Then tilt the bolt's northern end down about 60 degrees. (Earth's magnetic field is not parallel to the ground. It dips downward in the northern hemisphere.)

3. Jiggle the atoms in the bolt. Do this by striking the south end of the bolt sharply several times with a hammer (Figure 15a).

4. Bring one end of the bolt near the compass needle. You will see that the bolt has become a magnet. If it has not, strike it a few more times with the hammer.

What's Going On?

The atoms in a magnet are themselves tiny magnets all aligned in the same direction as shown in Figure 15b. In an iron bolt that is not a magnet, the atoms are arranged helter-skelter as seen in Figure 15c. If these unorganized atoms are jiggled in a magnetic field, they may align and turn the bolt into a magnet.

Keep Exploring—If You Have More Time!

- How can you change the magnetic bolt you made in Experiment 15 back into a nonmagnet?

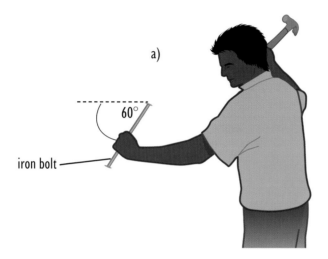

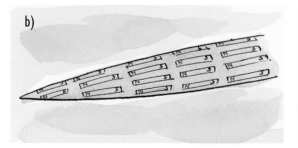

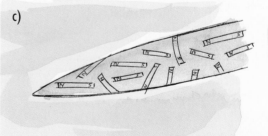

**Figure 15. a) Turn an iron bolt into a magnet by getting the atoms to line up in Earth's magnetic field.
b) The iron atoms in a magnet are themselves tiny magnets that are aligned north to south.
c) Iron atoms in a nonmagnet are disorderly arranged.**

16 Make a Simple Magnetic Motor

What's the Plan?

Let's make a simple magnetic motor.

WHAT YOU NEED:
- magnet
- magnetic compass

What You Do

1. Slowly bring the north pole of a magnet near the north pole of a magnetic compass. (The north pole of a compass needle is on the north end of the needle and points in a northerly direction.) You will see the compass needle start to spin as it is repelled (Figure 16).

2. Bring the magnet's north pole near the compass's north pole each time the compass needle points north. By carefully timing your movement of the magnet, you can keep the compass needle spinning. You have made a hand driven magnetic motor. It operates on the same principle as an electric motor.

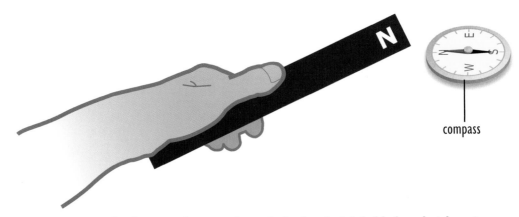

compass

Figure 16. A very simple magnetic motor shows the basic principle behind an electric motor.

What's Going On?

This experiment reveals the main principle that makes an electric motor work—the repulsion of like magnetic poles. In a real electric motor, one of the magnets is created by an electric current flowing in a coil of wires.

Keep Exploring—If You Have More Time!

- Put a magnetic compass in an aluminum pan and then in an iron pan. In which pan does the compass not work? Try to explain why it doesn't work. Will it work in a wooden bowl? In a glass dish?

17 Make a Magnetic Compass

What's the Plan?

Let's make a compass like the ones used by ancient sailors.

What You Do

1. Turn a sewing needle into a magnet. Use a magnet to stroke the entire length of the sewing needle. Always stroke the needle in the same direction with the same pole of the magnet (Figure 17a). Either pole (north or south) of the magnet can be used.

2. Cut off the bottom of a foam cup.

3. Nearly fill a plastic container with water.

4. Put the foam bottom on the water.

5. Place the needle on the foam (Figure 17b). Wait for the needle to stop moving. The north seeking end of your compass will point in a northerly direction. The other end will be the needle's south pole.

6. Slowly bring the north pole of a magnet near the north end of your compass. The north end will be repelled.

7. Bring the north pole of the magnet near the south pole of your compass. The south end will be attracted by the magnet.

> **WHAT YOU NEED:**
> - sewing needle
> - magnet
> - scissors
> - foam cup
> - plastic container
> - water

What's Going On?

Repeatedly stroking the steel needle with a magnet will force the iron atoms in the needle to line up in the same direction. (See Figures 15a and 15b.) Once many of the atoms are aligned, the needle becomes a magnet.

Keep Exploring—If You Have More Time!

- Make a variety of magnetic compasses from ordinary materials you can find in your home or school.

- Can you make a magnet from nails made of any metal? You might try steel, iron, aluminum, brass, lead, and copper.

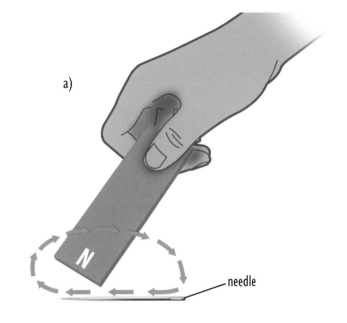

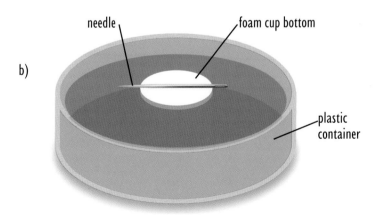

Figure 17. a) You can turn a sewing needle into a magnetic compass needle. b) Can you use your compass to find directions?

18 Bend a Stream of Water

What's the Plan?

Let's put electric charges on a comb and then use the comb to bend a stream of water.

WHAT YOU NEED:
- faucet
- sink
- plastic comb
- woolen cloth

What You Do

1. Adjust a faucet so that a very thin stream of water falls into a sink.

2. Use a plastic comb to briskly comb your hair.

3. Bring the end of the comb you used to comb your hair close to the thin stream of water (see Figure 18a). The stream of water will bend toward the comb.

4. Rub the comb with a woolen cloth.

5. Again, bring the comb near the thin stream of water. The stream will again bend toward the comb.

What's Going On?

Water molecules are polar (Figure 18b). One side of a water molecule is slightly positive; the other, slightly negative. So either a positively or a negatively charged comb will attract water molecules (Figure 18c). The attraction of the water molecules for the charged comb caused the stream to bend. Electric charges build up on objects rubbed with a cloth or hair. In dry air, charges collect on your body when you walk on a wool rug. On a larger scale, they accumulate on clouds, causing lightning.

Keep Exploring—If You Have More Time!

- Bring a charged comb near a thin stream of cooking oil. Are cooking oil molecules polar?

- Suspend a plastic ruler from a thread. Rub the ruler with a woolen cloth. Rub a second plastic ruler with the cloth. What will happen when you bring the second ruler close to the first one?

- Rub a glass test tube with a silk cloth. Bring the glass near the ruler you rubbed with wool. What happens? How do the charges on the glass compare with the charge on the ruler? If the wool is negatively charged, what charge is on the glass?

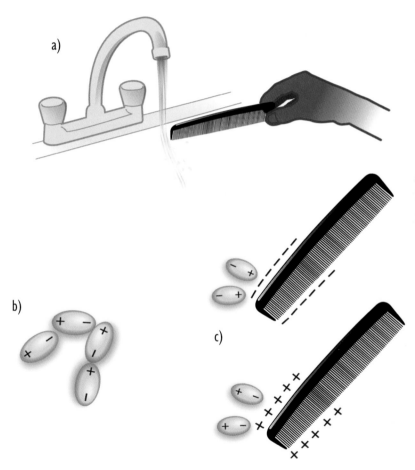

Figure 18. a) Bring a charged comb near a thin stream of water. b) Water molecules, shown here as ovals, are polar. c) Because water molecules are polar, they will be attracted to either positive or negative charges.

Words to Know

ammeter—An instrument (meter) used to measure electric current.

ampere—A unit of electric current. One ampere is a flow of charge equal to one coulomb per second or 6 1/4 billion billion electrons per second.

atom—The smallest particle of an element such as iron.

battery—A number of electric cells joined in series or in parallel that can provide an electric current.

conductors—Materials that will allow an electric current to pass through them.

D-cell—An electric cell that has a carbon rod (the positive electrode) in an electrolyte of powdered carbon mixed with manganese dioxide, ammonium chloride, and water. The entire cell is enclosed in a zinc can that serves as the negative electrode.

electric current—A flow of electric charge, usually along wires.

electric motor—A motor that consists of a wire coil that lies in a magnetic field. When an electric current flows through the coil, the repulsion of like magnetic poles causes the coil to spin and turn a shaft to which it is attached.

electrical resistance—The resistance to a flow of charges or the ratio of the voltage across a circuit element in an electric circuit to the current flowing through it.

electromagnet—A wire coil surrounding an iron core. The coil behaves like a magnet when electric current flows through it.

magnet—A true magnet attracts iron and certain other materials. It can both attract and repel another magnet.

magnetic compass—A small magnet that is free to turn. It can be used to find directions or to map a magnetic field.

magnetic field—The magnetic forces that surround a magnet. The directions of these forces can be mapped with compasses.

nonconductors—Materials that do not allow electric current to pass through them.

north-seeking magnetic pole or north magnetic pole—The end or side of a magnet that is attracted toward Earth's magnetic pole (a south-seeking pole) that is located in northern Canada.

parallel circuit—A circuit consisting of two or more circuit elements, such as light bulbs, connected side by side so that an electric current divides as it passes through the circuit.

resistor—A circuit element that is used to reduce electric current because it resists the flow of electric charges.

series circuit—A circuit consisting of two or more circuit elements, such as light bulbs, connected one after the other.

south-seeking magnetic pole or south magnetic pole—The end or side of a magnet that is repelled by Earth's magnetic pole (a south-seeking pole) that is located in northern Canada.

volt—A unit used to measure the energy given to electric charges by a battery or electric generator.

voltmeter—An instrument (meter) used to measure voltage.

Further Reading

Books

Bardhan-Quallen, Sudipta. *Championship Science Fair Projects: 100 Sure-to-Win Experiments*. New York: Sterling, 2007.

Drier, David Louis. *Electrical Circuits: Harnessing Electricity*. Mankato, Minn.: Compass Point Books, 2008.

Fairley, Peter. *Electricity and Magnetism*. Minneapolis, Minn.: Twenty-First Century Books, 2008.

Stringer, John. *Magnetism: An Investigation*. New York: PowerKids Press, 2008.

Woodford, Chris. *Experiments with Electricity and Magnetism*. New York: Gareth Stevens Publishers, 2010.

Internet Addresses

Electronics for Kids
    <users.stargate.net/~eit/kidspage.htm>

Electricity Unit
    <wow.osu.edu/experiments/electricity/eleclist.html>

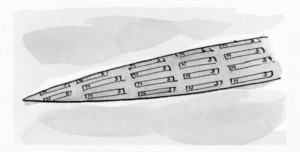

Index